I0221789

Divine
Detour

CHELLBEE JOHNSON

CHELLBEE JOHNSON

TABLE OF CONTENTS

CHELLBEE JOHNSON

Chains

"

Not that I have already obtained all this, or have already been made perfect, but I press on to take hold of that for which Christ Jesus took hold of me. Brothers, I do not consider myself yet to have taken hold of it. But one thing I do: Forgetting what is behind and straining toward what is ahead. Philippians 3:12-13

"

CHELLBEE JOHNSON

Dear Bold Believer Bestie,

There is no worse hurt than seeing your potential but
feeling suffocated by your past while trying to push
forward and become a better you. Even though you are
transitioning slowly, there are many things you no longer
do. Those closest to you seem not to understand.

I would love to tell you that walking with Christ is easy,
and everything will fall into place. However, the truth is
that is just not the case. As you continue walking forward
on this path of righteousness, you will learn many things.

Such as the person you became and believed in does not
align with the word of God. There will be days when part
of you will start to believe this new life with Christ isn't
possible for you. Bestie, I promise you it is. Day by day,
God will mold you, growing you into a mighty woman of
faith.

Just remember that this is a journey.

You must do the work of seeking God's face. Knowing
God, believing in the blood of Christ, and understanding
the power of the Holy Spirit will set you free from those
invisible chains.

Today, I want to challenge you to think about the new creation you have become.

- Read 2 Corinthians 5:16-17
- Who or what has made you feel ashamed, embarrassed, or uncomfortable with the new creation you are becoming in Christ? Maybe it was a slight word, unkind look, or less invites.
- Write down all the events and people that make you feel chained and like you shouldn't continue to change.
- Spend 15-30 minutes in prayer, and give your every hurt, fear, and chain to Jesus. Pray to forgive all those who have hurt you, as Christ forgives.

CHELLBEE JOHNSON

Mr. Right

I see it all so clearly
Short, fitted skirts, and platform pumps
Hoping to meet Mr. Right
Even if it's only for one night
Somehow it will help the time past
Until the next Saturday night

Overly ambiguous
An over achiever
Seeking validation
Hopelessly waiting
There is no debating
No mistaking

The hole in her heart
Hoping that love will spark
Light up every place that was dark
But waiting
To be chosen
By Mr. Right
Praying he will bring a new light
That he would set her path right
Her hope is in the wrong Mr. Right

Invisible Chains

Invisible bondage
Unseen fight
Unspoken hurt
That is so devasting
Causes you to begin contemplating
Your life's worth

How do I let go of the past?
I know they say hard times don't last
But what do you do when hard times is all you know

It's easy for them to tell you to just let it go
Because they don't know
All the pain, you've endured
The hurt that has left you scarred
The broken heart that has left you feeling like you're behind
bars

The chains of your past life
Those closest
Are a constant reminder and make you feel like you will never
be upright

Unable to make better choices
Hopeless
Worthless
Broken
Discarded
Far from chosen

CHELLBEE JOHNSON

Truly Be

How do I choose to believe, what God says about me?

Can I truly be
Chosen
Healed

When I look in the mirror
I see the wounds even clearer

Can I truly be
Victorious
Glorious

When I look at the current troubles
The future looks more like rubble

Can I truly be
Forgiven
Sinless

When I look at the past shortcoming
I see a tremendous distance from his glory

Can I truly be
A living testimony
Of His love, grace, and mercy

"

Do not call to mind the former things; pay no attention to the things of old.

Isaiah 43:18

"

CHELLBEE JOHNSON

Unseen Hurt

Pretty girl
Quiet smile
Upside down world
Unseen trials

No one sees the darkness of her past
Captured by her beauty
But unable to truly cast
Cast a relationship that last

A meaningful conversation

She is mysterious
Leaves everyone curious
What lies behind her smile
What hurt has defiled

Her once whole heart
So clearly broken
Although those words were never spoken

Unable to trust anyone
Fearful they could never understand
All she's seen or experienced

Uncertain Peace

My peace lay in this bottle
Unable to cope with the weight
Unknown fate

The feeling that I had made a mistake
Overwhelmed by anxiety
Uncertain future
Unopened doors
Unperceived intentions

My peace lay in this bottle
Unable to move forward
Unused gifts
Soul rifts

Unhinged grief
Unfounded belief

My peace lay in this bottle
Now it's empty

CHELLBEE JOHNSON

Unspoken Moments

It's often the unspoken hurt
The moments of friction
The difficult miscommunication

It's a missed opportunity
That creates resentment
Unrepentance

It's the quiet voice that says no one loves you
The uncelebrated wins
The self-serving friends

It's the misunderstanding
That becomes invisible chains
Quieting your natural tendencies

It's those brief moments
That are sharp
Shocking your heart
Unexpected
Leaving you second guessing
Yourself

These moments are often brief
But they feel as though they last an eternity

"

Because you neglected all my counsel, and wanted none of my correction.
Proverbs 1:25

"

CHELLBEE JOHNSON

Succumb to the Crowd

How do I go on
When I feel so alone
Why am I always left feeling wrong
Blaming myself
For cards I've been dealt

Why am I always left
Holding all the baggage
Filled with regret and shame
Convinced I am to blame
For choices I never made
Wishing there was something I could change

Convinced I should be
Ashamed of who I've become
Afraid I'll succumb
To presume to just go along
With the crowd even though I know their wrong

Believe and Receive

Frustrating
Debilitating
They love to see me waiting
There is no debating
Nor negating

That God has a plan for me
Even though it's hard to believe
I receive
And I intend to retrieve

Every gift that Christ said he would leave

For the lowly
And broken hearted
For those who at one point had departed
From the presence
The essence

Of our heavenly Abba Father
Adonai
Jehovah Rapha

CHELLBEE JOHNSON

Few are Chosen

Don't let them chain you
To their perception
Cause you to question
What God promised you

You know you were called
For a cause
For a time, such as this
A purposeful bliss

So often what they don't get
Is because of their ignorance
Many will wish

They were called
But few are willing to journey like apostle Paul
Giving they're all
To spread the gospel

"

I know your deeds. See, I have placed before you an open door, which no one can shut. For you have only a little strength, yet you have kept My word and have not denied My name.

Revelation 3:8

"

CHELLBEE JOHNSON

Life is too Short

Life is too short
to spend it worried about your opinion
Or explaining my intention
I must follow the call
Of God Almighty

Life is too short
To spend it wasting my days
Living it your way
I must follow the commands
Of God Almighty

Life is too short
To spend it with regrets
Worrying about your unmet
Expectations of me
I must follow the path
Of God Almighty

Life is too short
To spend it not doing God's work
Trying to explain my worth
Instead, I will put on the girth
The whole armor
Of my Abba Father

Gone

It's difficult to walk in boldness
When you have spent so much time shrinking
Over-thinking

Attaching your worth
To worthless words
Absurd

It's difficult to be authentic
When you're undone
True self gone

How am I to go on?
When all I once held clearly is gone

The status
The friends
The partying nights have come to an end

When there's no one there to mend
The broken
Heart
Shattering
Starts

How do you go on?
When everything you thought was important

CHELLBEE JOHNSON

Is gone

Tell the Truth

If I tell the truth
That His grace is sufficient
And there is nothing in life I'm missing
How His Spirit causes me to be different
To see I am gifted

They'll think I'm lying
Think I'm denying

If I tell the truth
Life had no roots
Based on worthless words
Arbitrary actions
Symbols & statuses
Attempts at becoming the main attraction
Obsessed with obsolete opulence
Wannabe women crush Wednesdays
Desperate for destructive
Video vixen lifestyle
Tainted by trivial traditions
Misguided mavens of the midnight
Void of values

"

Therefore if anyone is in Christ, he is a new creation. The old has passed away. Behold, the new has come!

2 Corinthians 5:17

"

CHELLBEE JOHNSON

They Wouldn't Believe

What will I say
Hey girl how's your day

Even hello
Is the beginning to the show
Dishing tea
Gossip
Nonstop nonsense
A whirlwind of words
Trivial passing of the time
Replay of the reality tv realm
Latest lovers
Slimming Surgeries
Wigs, weaves, and wonders

What a waste of the day
They would find it hard to believe that I would rather be
In His presence
Then under the trance of television

But I'm filled with so much joy
Because the one who created me
Fills me with incomprehensible joy
Even in my frustration
I'm patient
Because I trust Him

I have been

I've been disjointed
By disappointment
Given up on hope
Feeling alone
Destitute
Like my life is the butt of their jokes

I've been broken
Sunken
In a drunken
State of depression
Second guessing
My choices

I've been desperate
For love
Reprieve
Is all I need
From the emptiness
That nothing seems to feed

I've been bashed
By those closest
Bewildered
By broken trust
Caused me to question
Their first impression

CHELLBEE JOHNSON

Fool Me

Don't let them fool you
Into thinking
They believe
With the bearded words
And disguised eyes
They shout their shaded truth
But it's all lies

Weary of their
Willingness to assist
Expecting they will eventually
Dismiss
My thoughts
Which will only leave me lost

Futile feelings
To be dependent
On their validation

CHELLBEE JOHNSON

Forgiven

"

John the Baptist appeared in the wilderness, preaching a baptism of repentance for the forgiveness of sins.

Mark 1:4

"

CHELLBEE JOHNSON

Dear Bold Believer Bestie,

Sometimes, the hard part of this walk is letting go of your past. Look, I know you messed up in the past. The reality is you will likely mess up again.

God is a generous God with His love, mercy, and forgiveness. When he created Adam and Eve, he knew they would one day eat the fruit. From the beginning of his creation, God had a plan to reconcile us through the blood of Christ. He didn't create this plan because of the great things we did or will do but simply because of who He is.

He is Adonai, the great I Am that I Am, and the ultimate Creator who desires to commune with his creations. Put the weight of your shortcomings, sins, and failures down. Confess your sins to God every day and ask for forgiveness.

There is freedom when you recognize that you are saved only through Jesus Christ, whom you serve. No work of your own could have granted you His grace. He forgives you because he wants you back. I pray because your heart longs to be in constant connection, communication, and communion with God that you will extend forgiveness to your brothers and sisters when they fall, fail, or fool you. Remember, they are only humans like you. Offer forgiveness freely to all those you encounter.

Today, I want to challenge you to think about any unforgiveness you have been carrying.

- Read Mark 11:25-26
- What unforgiveness are you harboring that is affecting who you are and desire to be?
- What sins or shortcomings have you failed to confess to God?
- Set aside 15-30 minutes to pray using the A.C.T.S. Prayer Method
    o Adoration
    o Confession
    o Thanksgiving
    o Supplication

CHELLBEE JOHNSON

It Won't Cost You

God's forgiveness is free
See
We hold forgiveness hostage

I'll forgive if
I'll forgive you when

God is so gracious
He forgives you when
You were deep in sin

Jesus paid the cost
On the cross
Knowing he was saving the lost

I pray
That one day
I would say

I forgive you

No strings attached
No expectation of getting something returned back

Simply forgiving
To be more like Christ
In hopes I would become a light
Becoming a living sacrifice

It's Not Fair

It says forgive
And you will be forgiven

Lord, I don't know
How do I let go
Of all the hurt they caused
I can't ignore the scars
The so obvious flaws
The permanent damage of the word
The deep sorrow of feeling unheard

It just doesn't feel fair to me
Lord maybe I need therapy

Why should I have to forgive?

CHELLBEE JOHNSON

Love Like God

Forgive because He forgives
Forgive unselfishly
Forgive ambitiously
Forgive because you anticipate God's forgiveness

Forgive because unforgiveness is expensive
Unforgiveness is a forfeiture of the promises of God
Forgiving is not easy
Forgiving doesn't equal forgetting
Forgiving doesn't equal acceptance

Forgiving recognizes we are all flesh
Man will fail
The only perfection is in Christ and Christ alone
Forgiveness allows you to open your heart
Forgiveness frees you from bitterness
Most of all forgiveness allows you to love
Love as God loves

"

Be kind and tenderhearted to one another, forgiving each other just as in Christ God forgave you.

Ephesians 4:32

"

CHELLBEE JOHNSON

How do I forgive?

When nothing has changed
When their words still ring in my brain

When they took advantage of me
When I think they are Satan seeds

When they left me broken
When they left me hopeless

What almost took my life
What causes me to have sleepless nights

Lord, please tell me
How do I forgive?

An Unmastered Act

If I'm being honest
Forgiveness is an art I haven't mastered
Maybe it's why I often feel shattered
Broken into pieces
On a cold floor
Ready to meet death's door

When you're unwilling to forgive
It's difficult to live

A life reflective of Christ
Because you can't do it in your own right
See Christ was beaten, spat on, and hung
You know he did no wrong
Your forgiveness is the key
That will set you free
It will gather and mend
Making your heart whole again

CHELLBEE JOHNSON

It Costs

Unforgiveness has a cost
A bitterness
A hardness
To all who are lost

To you who think you can set terms
Make others earn

What do you desire to receive for free?
You need to understand forgiveness sets you free
When you forgive like Christ

Trust that he will make it all right
He will give you peace
Rise up in your healing power to release
Every heartache, hurt, and pain
So that you can become unstained

See He knows that it hurts
But he wants you to let it go
So that you can see Him at work

"

For if you forgive men their trespasses, your heavenly Father will also forgive you.

Matthew 6:14

"

CHELLBEE JOHNSON

Reconcile

What they said hurt
Made you question your worth
What if what was said was true?

The words are hard to reconcile
Which left my heart defiled
What do you do when those you love hurt you?
To be honest I have no clue

The truth is the words said
Says more about them than it does you
Holding onto those words
Only lend to the hurt
You have to forgive
Pray for them and the life they live

Skill

You took your
First step
That step of faith
The gift of salvation
Was the end to your pain
But baby it's only beginning
This walk is not easy
You will fall
You will get frustrated
But through it all know that
God is patiently waiting
Never debating
His love for you

Forgiveness is a skill
You require forgiveness, Lord
Because it provides a glimpse into who you are
I can't be more like you
Without becoming your attributes
Which are in your word
And the only truth

CHELLBEE JOHNSON

His Fruit

Like the branches of the tree
I should bear fruit that are easy to see
They should see your fruit
Joy
Peace
Love
Kindness
Faithfulness
Self-Control
Goodness
Patience

Forgiveness frees my soul
Can I say I'm yours while
Seeking vengeance
Being unrepentant
Being hateful
Being ungrateful
Having an adulterous heart
Giving up on everything I start
Wallowing in anxiety and worry
Being surly

"

Do not judge, and you will not be judged. Do not condemn, and you will not be condemned. Forgive, and you will be forgiven.

Luke 6:37

"

CHELLBEE JOHNSON

Burdens

It's hard to imagine
He knows my sins
Yet chooses to forgive them

How does he do it?

Look at my filth
Know my guilt
And yet He treats me with kindness
He asks me to be honest

To simply confess
All my mess
He tells me to lay it at the altar
Not to falter

Put my burdens down
Trust the power of His crown
Believe He can carry it all
Knowing no burden is too small

Don't pick it back up
Anxious and running a muck
Let Jesus carry it

Get Free

They say break every chain
Who unblots the stain

How do I get free?

I plead the blood
Yet I continue to feel stuck in the mud

How do I get free?

Free from the hurt of my past
Free from the remnants of my last
Free from everything they said I would never do
Free from the worldly wisdom I thought was true
Free from my sinful nature

CHELLBEE JOHNSON

Becoming an Empty Vessel

The hardest thing is the thought I could lose you
Misuse you
Abuse you

The hardest thing is desiring to be used by you
Scared I'll lose
Knowing I can't fool you
The hardest thing is being planted like a tree
Continually at your feet
Waiting to see what will be

The hardest thing is desiring to be your vessel
Finding myself in an uncharted battle but determined to
wrestle
Determined to endure the emptying of me

"

Bear with one another and forgive any complaint you may have against someone else. Forgive as the Lord forgave you.

Colossians 3:13

"

CHELLBEE JOHNSON

You Listen

You heard every prayer
Every cry
You were there

When I called out to you
In pain
You always ensured me it was not in vain

I knew I could come to you
And complain
Be unrestrained
Giving all my flaws to you
And walk away unstained

Unspoken petitions
Even those you listen

Simply because
You said
I am chosen

Your everlasting love
Generous grace
Which is more than enough

Seed on Unfertilized Soil

Before you can grow roots

They pluck you
Throw you away

Leave you spinning
Cause you to toil
It's when you realize you are on unfertilized soil

They sow more seeds
On polluted ground

Fill you with useless compliments
Baseless assumptions
Your heart is empty
You're unable to function

With no true identity
Limited understanding of your worth
Instead of seed
You feel more like dirt

CHELLBEE JOHNSON

They Will, But You Must Forgive

Much like the weeds
They hate to see you coming
Can't wait to see your shortcomings

They cheer you on
Expecting you won't go on
They don't expect to see you win
Secretly you know they aren't your friend

They will cut you
With their eyes
You know they're full of lies

They will cut you
With their words
And try to make you think you misheard

The thoughts they never spoke
But you often felt
They are not the dealer of the cards you were dealt
They will cut you
But you can't cut back
Or attack

Instead, you must
Forgive

CHELLBEE JOHNSON

Faith

"

Be doers of the word, and not hearers only. Otherwise, you are deceiving yourselves.

James 1:22

"

CHELLBEE JOHNSON

Dear Bold Believer Bestie,

Your faith is proportionate to your time with God. Many
have heard the word of God and are not believers. The
calling of a believer is to act in a way that aligns with the
word of God. If you do not know it, living out the word is
difficult. If you do not input the word of God into
yourself through

- Regular Bible study
- Wise counsel from biblically sound teachers and a
  strong community of believers
- Quiet time with God in prayer and meditation

Without the proper input, it will be difficult for you to live
a life that reflects His word. Romans 10:17 says that faith
comes by hearing, and hearing by the word of Christ. If
you feel a stunt in your faith and you're struggling to
believe the promises of God for His people, this could be
an indicator that you have

- Taken hold of false doctrine/teaching
- Ignorance of what the promises of God are
- The need to do a heart check in prayer

Often, the world encourages us to chase after material
things. Through that pursuit, we lose focus on the eternal
gifts of God, which include joy, peace, and love. Seeking
his hand instead of his heart is a common mistake
Christians make. Often, this leads to a life of strife,
disappointment, and confusion.

Reflect

Today, I want to challenge you to think about where your confidence is lying.

- Read Hebrews 11:1-3
- What is your hope in?
- What are you listening to and watching, and who are you surrounding yourself with?
- When you look at your output (your life), does it align with the word of God? Be honest with yourself and expect there will be some areas you will need to work on.

CHELLBEE JOHNSON

Lukewarm

Sunday service won't get it
You can't meditate on words you don't know
You can't pray something you don't know
You can't live a standard you're unaware of

Blissful ignorance is the same as willful disregard
You have a choice
You make it every day through your actions
In how you spend your time
In what you prioritize

This is my desperate cry
Please don't allow yourself to die
No one can afford
To be separated from the Lord

I beg you change now
You no longer have to be bound
By sin
Allow Christ to mend
All that's broken deep within
Read the word of God daily my friend

The Holy Spirit allows me to be the person
I always wanted to be
But never could be
In my own strength or power

His Change Requires You to Work

Don't be a cautionary tale
The one love always fails
Quick to anger
Slow to listen
Short on patience
Always faking
You have to do the work
Getting into God's word is about more than attending
church

CHELLBEE JOHNSON
Wait even when it's HARD

Lord let my
Faith Walk
Speak Louder
Than my
Faith talk

When the wait is long
Give me the strength to go on
Enlarge my faith
So that I may wait

Wait even when it's HARD
Renew the right spirit in me
Equipped to wait patiently

Humbly in
Anticipation
Reassured of your
Divine timing

"

For we walk by faith, not by sight.

2 Corinthians 5:7

"

CHELLBEE JOHNSON

The Spirit Transforms

When you get God's word in your heart
It will do its part
To take root in you
When God's word only lives in your mind
You're sure to find
Yourself frustrated at life's troubles
It's like a seed planted in rubble

Without the Holy Spirit
You're in trouble
The Holy Spirit will transform your heart
If you do your part
You'll no longer have to pretend
But instead start

To become the woman, you always wanted to be
Set free in God's beauty
Equipped with His power and authority

Vision

Now I finally get it
I never did understand
Never was able to see why I'm different
Because the vision
Isn't for them to see
It's strictly for me

It's like trying to teach an infant to read
Some things will just never be
God didn't call them to see this vision
This vision is strictly for me
They may see a faint line
A blurred dimension
But the fullness of the body
It's not for everybody

Lord forgive me
For limiting you
To only be the God others can see

CHELLBEE JOHNSON

His Presence

Your overwhelming presence
Lord I feel your essence
It's a blessing

But it's left me totally
And utterly
Out of my element

In the moments
When you come in
Knowing I needed a friend

Not to control me
But to console me

To remind me
How deep your love
Flows for me

It perplexes me
I don't understand how this could be
How you love me
Even though you see all of me

"

Now faith is the assurance of what we hope for and the certainty of what we do not see.

Hebrews 11:1

"

CHELLBEE JOHNSON

The Bible is a Love Letter

Don't take my word for it
Girl, you need to know it
Know the feel of its page
The gaze eyes
And daring glazes
The trembling in his presence
The shout that erupts from his essence

The open love letters
Instructions
In hopes you do better

The prayer that you would try again
The reminder you have a friend

Most beautiful depiction
You'll ever read
The love letter from our home
In heaven
We all need

Not all answer His Call

The boldness
The bond

The lost
Now found
The dim
The brim
The lame
Now unashamed

The fall
The call
Not all
Will have the gall
To stand tall

Enter his gates
Take their place
This you can't fake
His children
Know their fate

CHELLBEE JOHNSON

Jesus loves you

Let me pray
With you
Lay with you
Stay with you
Hold you

No I don't want to control you
I owe you
Every promise
You were told
Believe them, be bold

Many have been told
But not all were sold
Willing to enter the fold
I gave my life on a tree
In hopes that one day you would be
Reconciled through faith
Refusing Satan's bait

"

Consequently, faith comes by hearing, and hearing by the word of Christ.

Romans 10:17

"

CHELLBEE JOHNSON

Your Unmerited Favor

Forgive me Lord for ever
Doubting the gifts, you sent
Your favor, grace, and mercy endure forever

Even though we don't deserve it
You grant us favor
Because you deemed your creations as worth it
Your love for us does not waver

Thank you Lord for your love
You give generously
It is so clearly from above
Perfect and enduring
Patient and reassuring

You are my constant help
Staying with me when I'm beside myself
Your grace is an unmerited gift
Only you can transform and lift

What many deemed as broken
And hopeless
You give your word
To guide us and realign our focus

Thank you for guiding
My limited and often binding
Understanding of who you are
Your love stretches so far

Adjusting for the Room

When it's not easy to walk into every room as yourself
Because every time you enter you have to check
Who's in the room
To ensure you adjust your views
To fit that crowd
Not be labeled as loud

Don't be too animated, look humble and not proud
Hide behind smiles and cliché sayings that aren't worth
while

Making sure everyone is comfortable
Let me make sure I'm appropriate
Wrestling with knowing that your full self in this room
Would be labeled as hood, ratchet, ghetto, anything but
professional
Questionable
At best

CHELLBEE JOHNSON

The unconscious shift

The shift, subtle yet swift
In your posture
Pronunciation of every word proper
The desperate attempt, to ensure they don't label you
As ill-equipped
An unqualified misfit

"

And without faith it is impossible to please God, because anyone who approaches Him must believe that He exists and that He rewards those who earnestly seek Him.

Hebrews 11:6

"

CHELLBEE JOHNSON

Choosing Freedom

If I try to be everything
To everybody
I'll end up being nothing to myself
A shell
A slave
To your opinion
A fake
A snake
You'll slither on about your way

Leaving me to carry the shame
Too often I have taken the blame

So now I choose to abstain
I have nothing to gain
So I reframe
No longer ashamed

I'm sorry

I'm sorry
My mission
Doesn't fit your limited vision
Of me and who I was created to be

I'm sorry
I will do a lot of things
But I will never apologize for following the call of God
I'm sorry
That I'm not sorry

Because for once in my life I walked in boldness
That could have only been the Holy Spirit
I'm sorry
But I refuse to keep hiding
I refuse to be anything less than the purpose that God has
for me

CHELLBEE JOHNSON

They

I don't think they get me
They won't let me be
If I walk in the room
And I'm not filled with gloom

They'll think I'm fronting
It will only leave them wondering
What's really wrong
What's going on

There's no way she could be happy

CHELLBEE JOHNSON

Surviving
Trials

"

Blessed is the man who perseveres under trial, because when he has stood the test, he will receive the crown of life that God has promised to those who love Him.

James 1:12

"

CHELLBEE JOHNSON

Dear Bold Believer Bestie,

I haven't written enough books to describe all the trials
God has brought me through. I believe your testimony is
the same. Time after time, Christ has pulled you out of
dark places, circumstances, and tribulations.

His hand has continually been on you, reminding you of
His love for you. James 1:2 says, "Consider it pure joy, my
brothers, when you encounter trials of many kinds." We
know that our trial enables us to mature spiritually that
maturity allows us to bear the fruits of the Holy Spirit's
patience, kindness, and peace.

Many times during our troubles, we want to distance
ourselves from God. We don't want to bring him into our
mess. But failing to go to the Father with your trials,
shortcomings, and burdens is one of the biggest mistakes
you can make. I hate to be the one to tell you, but it is
likely a sin.

Pride often leads us to think that we can carry the weight
of our burdens on our own. But the word is clear when it
says you are to cast your burdens on Him because he cares
for you. Moreover, He knows you can't carry it on your
own. The Father knows in all His sovereignty that your
attempt to carry your burdens would destroy your ability
to bask in His peace and joy.

Only in our relationship with Christ can we experience His
perfect peace that surpasses our understanding. So, in your

trouble, draw near to God. Allow your trouble to triage you into the divine care and comforter God.

Amid your trial, I want you to challenge yourself to praise God. I know you are uncertain of the outcome, but in your outcry to the Father, I dare you to thank Him now for the deliverance, restoration, and peace He is bringing to that circumstance. In that trouble, He is going to reveal some things to you. He will develop your character when you let Him, and you will walk in His light. No matter what comes your way.

Today, I want to challenge you to think about what burdens you carry.
- Read James 1:2-8
- Why haven't you laid your burden(s) at the feet of Christ?
- Reflect on who you are. Why do you feel it is necessary to deal with or face this burden apart from Christ? Often, pride, fear, desire for control, or even shame cause us to attempt to hide our burdens from Christ.

CHELLBEE JOHNSON

God can use it

Don't hold onto your past
As a way to stay hurt
As an excuse to stay broken

Give your past pain, hurt, and failure
To Adonai
For His grace is sufficient
God can use your past hurt

That heartache
That mistake
It is never too late

When God steps in and gives His grace
Your pain will become a reminder of His goodness

His perfect provision
In every trial and test
You can rest
For Adonai knows best

Hand or Heart

Do you want his hands
Or do you want his heart
The question he asks us all at the start

In every trial and tribulation
You are to count it all joy

You can have joy
Because you're in his presence
You smell his Holy Essence

Although the darkness obscures your view
You know His voice and are not confused
By the dark one's ruse

The storm may rock your boat
But you know He is your present help

You're calm
Knowing you're always in His palm

CHELLBEE JOHNSON

Rejoice Always

My peace
My joy
You can't destroy

You can't shake me
You can't break me
And you most definitely didn't make me

My newfound voice
My realization that I have a choice
I now continuously rejoice

It doesn't matter what trouble comes
Even in the thick of the storm I am not overcome
By the soul stealing demons that once left me succumb

"

You will be hated by everyone because of My name, but the one who perseveres to the end will be saved.

Matthew 10:22

"

CHELLBEE JOHNSON
Chaos and Confusion

God I am so hurt
I'm offended
I'm frustrated
I'm confused

I planted myself on the solid rock
On your firm foundation

But when I look around
I find myself surrounded
By chaos and confusion

Darkness often tries to overtake
Tries to make me

Go against your word
Tries to bend my will

Even in my submission to you
These battles leave me mentally exhausted
Distracted from my calling

The Storm

When the rain is heavy from the storm
When the waves swarm
The path ahead is unclear
The end feels as though it is near

Gasping for breath
Not sure if there is much life left
Give me the strength to persevere
With you there is no need to fear

Even when the waves are blinding
Lord you're beside me
When it's dark and I feel out of place
You give me the strength to endure the race

When the screams of the wind
Leave me unable to fend
For myself
You are my present help

CHELLBEE JOHNSON

A Friend in Jesus

Weary
Worried
Tired of seeing another success story

Lord when is it going to happen for me

I don't want to be selfish
I'm trying not to complain
But where are you in this pain
That seems to be my life

Where is my blessing
My second helping
Lord this is not what I was expecting
You said your promises are yes and amen
Lord can you at least send me a friend

"

In the day of prosperity, be joyful, but in the day of adversity, consider this: God has made one of these along with the other, so that a man cannot discover anything that will come after him.

Ecclesiastes 7:14

"

CHELLBEE JOHNSON

You are Blessed

You don't have to rush to the destination
It's waiting for you
Nobody can take it
When it arrives, nobody will mistake it

For anything less than an act of God
Many will shake their head and nod
Cheer you on
Surprised that they were wrong

Because they couldn't see
All that God created you to be

Many have jeered
Have attempted to steer
You in a different direction
Because of their misperception
Who you are, is nothing short of a blessing

Unlocking the Prophetic

You said it
You don't need to regret it
The new thing God is doing
I know the conversation left you stewing
Your mind is brewing

The prophecy
The prodigy
Unlocking His philosophy

The inner transformation
The unlocked imagination
Visions and dreams
Prophetic gleams

Into the coalesce of your purpose
It may make you nervous
But you have been called to service
The Most High
El Shaddai

It's hard to imagine they don't agree
How could they not see
All the one true God Almighty
Created you to be

CHELLBEE JOHNSON

Obedience to the Still Voice

When God wants to use you
There will be nothing you can do

He is unstoppable

When you're his willing vessel
You will no longer wrestle

The Holy Spirit
His voice will be audible
It may seem illogical

But he speaks
If you're willing to listen
His wisdom and knowledge is given
Freely to all who seek

His still voice
Gives no choice
You will become obsessed with obedience

"

Not only that, but we also rejoice in our sufferings, because we know that suffering produces perseverance; perseverance, character; and character, hope.
Romans 5:3-4

"

CHELLBEE JOHNSON

God's Love

A showing of His favor
His love for you
When that day comes be sure you savor

This is your reminder that even now
Many will doubt unsure of how

You were chosen
Thinking you are far from a token

But his love for you runs deep
When you feel it makes you weak

He will renew you
Often subdue you
With his
Unmerited
Unchanging
Unconditional
Love

Endure in Christ

They lied
When they said I'd be alright
That all I had to do is trust in you
But it's so much more to the story
You've got me exploring

How to be a better person
One worthy
Of your calling
Lord I'm all in

When I fall short of your glory
Help my vision to not become blurry
Remind me of your perfect mercy and grace
Strengthen me in Christ to endure this race

CHELLBEE JOHNSON

Rooted Word

Is the word rooted in you
Or is it like a pebble
That is tossed around

Is the word rooted in you
Or is it like a leaf
In fall
Dead
Leaving the branches bare

Is the word rooted in you
Or is it like a rotted branch
Withering
Broken

"

Blessed is the man who perseveres under trial, because when he has stood the test, he will receive the crown of life that God has promised to those who love Him.
James 1:12

"

CHELLBEE JOHNSON

Take Root

If the word is rooted in you
It will be like a tree
Still
Strong
Steady
Holding on

If the word is rooted in you
It will be like an anchor
It may drift
But it won't lift
When the waves of life appear
It will remain near

If the word is rooted in you
It will be like a lake
Gently swayed
By the waves
But the body remains
The same

Dim

Devastated
Jagged
Frustrated
Dragging my feet every step of the way
In complete dismay
Ready to go astray

Walking with Him didn't seem to pay
Hit after hit
Day after day
Seeking Him
And doing things his way
What do you do when you seek his heart
And your future looks dark?

CHELLBEE JOHNSON

The Source

Who's your source
Many will report
They are believers in our Lord
Our Father & Savior Jesus Christ

But when we look at their life
Christ like
Is far from what they exemplify

Many will say this faith walk
Is not about perfection
Then launch into a lot of grace talk

Hebrews 10 is clear
If you knowingly sin
You will meet a predetermined end

For God's wrath and fury
Is inescapable

CHELLBEE JOHNSON

Bearing
Fruits

"

But the fruit of the Spirit is love, joy, peace, patience, kindness, goodness, faithfulness, gentleness, and self-control. Against such things there is no law.

Galatians 5:22-23

"

CHELLBEE JOHNSON

Dear Bold Believer Bestie,

Being a Christian is work. There are no ifs, ands, or buts about it. Simply holding the title without transformation is deceptive but mostly un-Christ-like.

When you look at the life of Christ, it is easy to say he is the Son of God, perfect in all his ways and without sin. How could I possibly be like Him? Christ is not our only example of being Christ-like.

Look at the Apostle Paul; he was a persecutor of early Christians. An encounter with Jesus transformed him. He became the primary writer for much of the New Testament, even from prison. Paul was just a man like you and me, but he allowed his encounter with Jesus to transform Him.

You can have that same transformation. When you receive the Holy Spirit, He transforms you. You hear differently, see differently, your heart changes and your capacity to love grows.

John 13:35 says, "By this everyone will know that you are My disciples, if you love one another." Matthew 22:39 says, "Love your neighbor as yourself." Maybe you have not begun to read your bible, pray, or attend church regularly. When you look at your transformation, have you allowed Christ in your heart so that you can love others in a way that is Christ-like?

Bestie, I pray you will hear my heart when I say this. This walk with Christ is a journey. Your transformation will not happen overnight. As you continue the journey, submit to Christ, ask for wisdom, and seek diligently after God. He will make you a new creation that the world will despise because it does not love Jesus Christ.

Reflect
Today, I want to challenge you to truly look at your faith walk.

- Read James 1:19-27
- When you started your walk with Christ, where and how did you spend most of your time?
- Consider how long you have been walking with Christ. How have your routine, friends, and desires changed?

CHELLBEE JOHNSON

Gift of Grace

You are not called to conform
Don't get distracted by the norm
In the midst of the storm
Many will judge you in an attempt to reform

Your solid foundation
Don't let them cause you to forget you are a part of
Abraham's generation
Impeccable faith
That must not be disgraced

Thank you Jesus that your blood paid the price
No longer required to sacrifice
Unblemished animals for our sins
Now you look within

Our heart
Patiently awaiting
Generous love and grace
Which covered us from the start

Rooted in Him

He wants you to be rooted in his word
Not because He wants to bury you deep in the dirt
But because He knows His soil
Will give you a strong foundation
One that won't leave you wavering
It is only natural for you to assimilate
By the world's indoctrination

Like a seed planted on fertile ground
With nourishment you'll spring up
God wants to nourish you

Because he knows that if the world is your source
You will conform
Shallow roots, a weak seedling unable to thrive
You'll be tossed from side to side

With Christ as your source
Your roots are firmly planted
You won't be tempted to fit in
Because of his light
You will stand out
That I do not doubt

CHELLBEE JOHNSON

Pursue Him Relentlessly

Be unrelenting in your pursuit of Christ
Because the better you know him
The more you will be able to see

Your true identity
Beyond the words from others
Outside of your circumstances
Overcoming the limitations of your current situation

When Christ shows you who you are
It elevates your identity in a way
That enables you to be the best version of yourself

You won't look to impress others
You won't seek to be like the rest
You'll see you don't need the validation

You will walk in the knowing of his every call
You no longer worry that you will fall
You will trust that God has seen you through

Every tear and fear
Year after year
Has you in His perfectly capable hands
His promise and his plans
For you are near
Trust Him my dear

"

I am the vine and you are the branches. The one who remains in Me, and I in him, will bear much fruit. For apart from Me you can do nothing.
John 15:5

"

CHELLBEE JOHNSON

My Worship is Real

Worship him for every time they told you, you were
nothing
Every time they didn't invite you
Evey time they told you, you would never make it
Every time they said you were weird
Every time they said you were nobody
Every time they said you were ugly
Every time they said you were worthless

This praise is only for those who have been rejected
Those who know they should be dead or in jail
Those who went to hell and back
Those who have been disappointed
Those who have been broken hearted
Those who have been discarded
But look unsinged

Those who gave up
But God came
And gave them a hand
Picked them up again and again

Cherish your Testimony

Don't you dare let them make you feel like
You need to hide from your past
Cherish every shortcoming
He brought you through
Your testimony is the physical embodiment
Of God's triumph
When you were filthy rags
He was willing to pick you up and take you back

He chose you
You better know he loves you
Not because of what you can do
But because you're His
He doesn't need you
But He wants you
Isn't it a feeling to be wanted even though you're not
needed

CHELLBEE JOHNSON

The Majestic Wonder of How He Uses You

I used to cry
Out of shame
Out of a broken place

See I didn't know I had been chosen
Didn't know I was being molded
I couldn't have imagined

He would use my every tear
To help bring someone else near
To Him

See just how good he is
Nothing you go through goes unnoticed
He has laser focus

In all his majestic wonder
He somehow manages to bring us from down under

"

So that you may walk in a manner worthy of the Lord and may please Him in every way: bearing fruit in every good work, growing in the knowledge of God.

Colossians 1:10

"

CHELLBEE JOHNSON

Becoming a Worshipper

Your tears are going to change
Your worship is becoming who you are
His praise is going to be constantly on your lips
People are going to see your light even when your lips are
zipped

God's voice is going to be audible
His presence is going to be palpable
You're going to yearn for his presence
You'll find His essence

Now He has become the source of your joy
Satan is going to have to come at you different
Your constant armor for warfare is going to be
Your calm in strife and the storm
Worship becomes your norm

He makes Crooked Paths Straight

You can't afford to forget about all God has done for you
How dare you only thank him for breath
When he got you out of that mess
With your ex

When he pulled you out of that depression
That had you second guessing
If you wanted to live
What you had to give

The memories you couldn't digest
The ones that you kept regurgitating unable to forget
The childish ways
The wrong turns and bad days

Unguided youth on crooked paths
Thoughts this brighter day won't last
Fear of spotlights on your mistakes
Worried that your salvation has come too late

CHELLBEE JOHNSON

Hate like Him

You will allow it around you
If you don't hate it
You will condone it

If you don't hate it
You will conform to it
If you don't hate it
You will do it
If you don't hate it

There is no room for indifference
There is no room for impartiality
You either love what God loves
Hating what God hates

Or you make yourself an enemy of God
And a lover of the world
You were not created to love this world
You were created by the Creator

Who desires you
Who loves you
Who longs to be loved by His creations

"

For the fruit of the light consists in all goodness, righteousness, and truth.

Ephesians 5:9

"

CHELLBEE JOHNSON

Peace

Holding onto it, you know there's a void
You desperately desire to fill
You look for ways to build
A new life

But no matter what you do
You seem to come up empty
Hopeless and without a clue
I want to tell you what I wish I knew
The void
The emptiness
The failure
The violation
The abuse
The misuse

It's all a sham
Nothing compares to the precious lamb
The new start
You desire
The mark
You want to make
Can only be accomplished
When you give your life
To Christ
Allow him in truly
And fully
His living water
Will fill every empty space

His Presence

Simply overwhelmed
By your presence
Just to feel your essence
It's something
I deeply cherish
A gift that is simply a blessing

Those quiet moments of reflection
Where you reveal your perception
In the secret place
Where I await
Your presence

Praise you endlessly
Until I am completely empty
Pouring it all out
Casting out all doubt

CHELLBEE JOHNSON

Let Them See You

Overflow
Breakthrough
Less of me
Lord more of you

Mold me
Hold me
Pour me all out
Show me what loving you is all about

Outpour your love
It's pure and from above
Cause them to see none of me
And all of you
So they may experience love like this, pure and true

"

Likewise, every good tree bears good fruit, but a bad tree bears bad fruit.

Matthew 7:17

"

CHELLBEE JOHNSON

Your Salvation

I would rather you know
Christ Jesus
I would rather you
Be in a relationship with God

I would rather you
Submit yourself to the Lord
I would rather you
Love the Lord wholeheartedly

Unreservedly
With all you have
Your salvation is the only thing that will last

Jehovah Nissi

Oh Adonai
How I love you
I worship and adore you
How you bring me joy
To simply speak your name
Oh how it brightens my day
You are wonderful
In all your ways
Your majesty
Eludes me

Thank you Lord for who you are
My foundation
My refuge
My fortress
My helper in times of distress
My protector in danger
My army when I am under attack
You always have my back

CHELLBEE JOHNSON

New Day with Christ

When I think of all you've done
All the battles you've won
I know there's nothing I can't overcome

You turn my darkest night
Into your light
My shortcoming
Becomes your testimony
Of how you save the despaired
And even the impaired

You give them all a second chance
With never a second glance
At all their faults
Despite all they thought they lost

Their repentant hearts
Prayers for a new start

You hear
And make this one thing very clear
Their sins have been washed away
The blood of Christ brings light to a bright new day

THANK YOU

Thank you for allowing me to be a part of this reflective journey with you. I pray that you can cherish the many mindset shifts God has brought you through. While eagerly anticipating the future shifts that are to come.

If you are anything like me, this journey felt like relief, joy, sadness, gratitude, reflection, and potentially some cringe-worthy moments of the work ahead of you.

Prayerfully, this has been an experience that brought peace and validated those moments of hurt and shortcomings. Glorify God for the many triumphs. I pray you will stay curious and open about how the Holy Spirit is seeking to teach you in each season.

Bold Believer Bestie, if you want to continue the journey with me, subscribe to the Dear Bold Believer YouTube channel for a big Bold cup of Christ every Monday at youtube.com/@chellbee

I love you. Be Bold, Be Blessed!

Chellbee Johnson

CHELLBEE JOHNSON

OTHER BOOKS

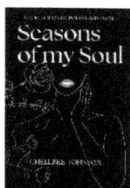

SEASONS OF MY SOUL
A COLLECTION OF POETRY AND
PROSE

ENCOURAGED
A 21 DAY REAL TALK DEVOTIONAL

WOMAN, YOU ARE SET FREE
A 31-DAY BIBLE STUDY JOURNAL

BLEMISHED BUT BEAUTIFUL
A 30-DAY GUIDED BIBLE STUDY
JOURNAL FOR WOMEN

Available everywhere books are sold in
paperback. You can also purchase on
www.dearboldbeliever.com

ABOUT THE AUTHOR

Chellbee Johnson is an Author, Bible Teacher, CEO of Dear Bold Believer, and Co-Founder of Bible Beauty Co.

She encourages everyday women to boldly pursue a life after Christ. As a wife and mom of 2, she inspires women to stay connected to the word of God despite life's busyness.

She was raised in Compton, California by a single mother. A latchkey kid, she often was left to care for herself. As a middle child, she felt unseen, which fueled her desire for acceptance and resulted in her pursuit of perfection and worldly success.

Despite graduating Summa Cum Laude with a master's in health service administration, she found herself crushed by life when she failed at corporate America.

In her darkest hour, after a demotion at work, she found refuge with Christ and reconciled herself to Him in 2016. Prayerful that Christ could heal her brokenness. She became a self-taught bible student, determined to help other women chase after the word of God. There is no way she could have made it from average woman to extraordinary without the love and salvation of Christ Jesus.

YOUTUBE

@chellbee

INSTAGRAM

@dearboldbeliever

PINTEREST

@iamchellbee

FACEBOOK

@dearboldbeliever

Copyright © 2024 by Dear Bold Believer LLC
All rights reserved. No part of this publication may be reproduced,
stored, or transmitted in any form or by any means, electronic,
mechanical, photocopying, recording, scanning, or otherwise, except
as permitted under Section 107 or 108 of the 1976 United States
Copyright Act, without the prior written permission of the author.
Requests to the author and publisher for permission should be
addressed to the following email: ChellBee@dearboldbeliever.com.

Scripture quotations taken from The Holy Bible, Berean Standard
Bible, BSB is produced in cooperation with Bible Hub, Discovery
Bible, OpenBible.com, and the Berean Bible Translation Committee.
This text of God's Word has been dedicated to the public domain.

www.dearboldbeliever.com

ISBN: 979-8-9902163-0-3

Editor: Priscilla J Henley

Cover Art and Interior Design: Chellbee Johnson

Author Photo: Justin Harrell

www.ingramcontent.com/pod-product-compliance
Lightning Source LLC
Chambersburg PA
CBHW070458090426
42735CB00012B/2608